AF377754

THE ESSENCE OF

Ferrari

UNFOLDED

CON

TENT

THE
HISTO

1

ENZO FERRARI

THE LEGACY OF ENZO FERRARI

"ALL FACTORIES ARE MADE OF MACHINES, walls, and people. I believe Ferrari is made of people first and foremost."

This conviction defined Enzo Ferrari—and shaped everything that followed.
Ferrari is more than a symbol of speed or luxury. It is a testament to Italian ingenuity, perseverance, and belief. From modest beginnings, Enzo Ferrari built not simply a company, but a vision—one driven by competition, innovation, and an unrelenting desire to excel. In doing so, he transformed the city of Modena and left a mark on Italian industry that endures to this day.

THE ORIGINS OF THAT VISION CAN BE TRACED TO 1908, when Enzo's father took him to watch the Coppa Florio near Bologna. Amid the dust, noise, and danger of early motor racing, something ignited. What Enzo saw was not merely a spectacle, but a calling. Racing revealed itself as both risk and purpose—a place where courage, skill, and identity converged.

In those years, racing drivers were modern heroes. Their victories promised immortality, their failures exacted a brutal cost. Enzo absorbed these ideals deeply, combining his growing passion for racing with practical experience gained in his father's workshop. Yet history would not grant him an easy path.

The First World War shattered the Ferrari family. Enzo was conscripted, fell gravely ill, and narrowly survived. His father and brother did not. Alone and grieving, Enzo emerged from the war with little more than resolve. Rejected by Fiat, the dominant force in Italian motoring, he faced a defining moment of despair—one he later recalled with painful clarity. Yet rejection did not break him. It sharpened him.

In 1919, Enzo finally entered competition, racing first for CMN and later Isotta Fraschini. Results were modest, but progress was real. He raced relentlessly, driven less by trophies than by belonging. For Enzo, competition was life itself. As he famously observed, "Second place is only the first of the losers."

His turning point came with Alfa Romeo. There, Enzo matured as a driver and emerged as a respected figure within Italian motorsport. Victory at the Coppa Acerbo in 1924 confirmed his ability, but an earlier moment would prove even more symbolic. In 1923, after a win at the Savio Circuit, Enzo was gifted the emblem of the prancing horse

FIRST RACE

In 1919 Enzo Ferrari completed his first ever race - the Parma-Poggio di Bercato hillclimb.

by the mother of war hero Francesco Baracca. He adopted it as his own—a symbol of courage, honor, and destiny.

By the late 1920s, Enzo's ambitions had evolved. In 1929, he founded Scuderia Ferrari, initially as a racing arm supporting Alfa Romeo. It was not yet a car manufacturer, but it was the foundation of something greater. Ferrari the brand would follow in 1947, but Ferrari the idea had already taken shape.

Enzo Ferrari's legacy does not rest on individual victories or machines. It lives in a philosophy—one forged through loss, perseverance, and belief. A belief that racing was not an end in itself, but a means to express excellence.

"I hope the red cars bearing my name will continue to exist after I am gone," he once said.

They do—not only as machines, but as carriers of a dream that began with one man, and continues to move the world.

FERRARI IN FORMULA I, 1951

THE BIRTH OF FERRARI

"THE PERFECT RACING CAR is the one that breaks down a moment after the finish line."
— Enzo Ferrari

Ferrari's rise to global authority in motorsport was neither smooth nor inevitable.

Long before the marque became synonymous with dominance and desire, its foundations were shaped by conflict, loss, and interruption. The birth of Ferrari was not a clean beginning, but a process of survival.

In 1929, Enzo Ferrari founded Scuderia Ferrari as a racing arm for Alfa Romeo. At first, Ferrari was not a manufacturer but a custodian—organizing, preparing, and running Alfa Romeo race cars. Motorsport was the language through which Enzo expressed both ambition and identity.

THAT RELATIONSHIP, HOWEVER, GREW STRAINED. By 1939, conflicts within Alfa Romeo led Enzo to depart. Bound by contract, he was forbidden from using his own name in competition for five years. In response, he founded Auto Avio Costruzioni, a company operating in exile from its own identity. In 1940, it built two racing cars for the Mille Miglia. Neither finished. It was a symbolic failure— ambitious, courageous, and unresolved.

Then came war.

During World War II, the factory's focus shifted to wartime production. In 1944, Allied bombings destroyed the facilities entirely. What remained was rubble, uncertainty, and resolve. By 1945, Enzo had rebuilt. When the naming restrictions finally expired, he acted decisively. In 1947, Auto Costruzioni Ferrari was officially founded. Ferrari, at last, could exist in name as well as spirit.

On March 12, 1947, the first Ferrari engine was started. The car was the 125 S. Enzo, unimpressed by its early form, nicknamed it "Autobotte"—the fuel truck. Yet this imperfect machine carried the future. Driven by Franco Cortese, it debuted at Piacenza on May 11. Mechanical failure ended the race early. Two weeks later, the same car returned and won in Rome.

Momentum followed quickly. On July 13, 1947, the two 125 S cars achieved a one-two finish at Parma, with Tazio Nuvolari and Cortese leading the field. In a move that revealed Enzo's pragmatism, both cars were dismantled. Their components were reused to build the next generation—machines designed not for preservation, but progress.

Ferrari's ascent continued steadily, but the defining moment arrived in 1951 at the British Grand Prix at Silverstone. Ferrari faced Alfa Romeo directly, with Juan Manuel Fangio leading the opposition. In a race decided by a fraction of a second, José Froilán González crossed the line ahead, securing Ferrari's first Formula One victory.

The win marked a symbolic rupture. Alfa Romeo soon withdrew from racing altogether. Ferrari had surpassed its origin.

Enzo later described the moment with painful clarity: triumph intertwined with loss, victory shadowed by gratitude and guilt. It was not merely a win—it was independence.

From that point forward, Ferrari stood alone. The 1950s would bring fierce rivalries, especially with Maserati, but Ferrari's position was secured. Born from adversity, shaped by war, and forged in competition, Ferrari emerged not as an imitation of greatness—but as its successor.

The birth of Ferrari was not a single moment. It was an act of endurance.

FLAVIO MANZONI, CHIEF DESIGN OFFICER

FERRARI'S DESIGN PHILOSOPHY

FERRARI DESIGN DOES NOT BEGIN WITH A FINISHED FORM. It begins with an idea—often fragile, often incomplete—captured in a line drawn quickly across paper. From that first gesture to the finished car, the process is one of refinement rather than invention, of discipline rather than spectacle.

At the center of this process is Ferrari's Centro Stile in Maranello. More than a design department, it is the intellectual heart of Ferrari, where designers, engineers, and craftsmen work in constant dialogue. Here, tradition is not preserved by repetition, but by interpretation.

TODAY, THAT DIALOGUE IS GUIDED BY Flavio Manzoni, Ferrari's Chief Design Officer. Under his direction, Ferrari has brought design fully in-house, ensuring that form, performance, and identity are conceived as a single idea rather than separate disciplines. Innovation, at Ferrari, is never detached from memory. The past is not quoted—it is absorbed.

The creation of a new Ferrari is deliberately slow. While many cars move from sketch to production in weeks, a Ferrari may take years. The reason is balance. Every surface must serve multiple purposes: visual tension, aerodynamic efficiency, and emotional clarity. Nothing is allowed to exist for decoration alone.

Despite advanced digital tools, hand drawing remains essential. For Manzoni, drawing is not nostalgia but necessity—the most direct connection between thought and form. Only once an idea is fully understood on paper does it migrate into digital space, where it is refined through complex modeling and simulation.

FERRARI 250 GTO

YET THE MOST REVEALING STAGE REMAINS PHYSICAL. Full-scale clay models are shaped over metal frames, first by robotic milling and then by hand. Designers sculpt surfaces millimeter by millimeter, chasing light, proportion, and flow. Clay, in this context, is not primitive—it is precise. It allows designers to see what software cannot: how a car truly occupies space.

These models are combined with polymer components produced through advanced manufacturing, then coated to evaluate color and reflection. Only when form and light align does the design move forward, scanned and transformed once again into data. The process is cyclical, not linear.

Aerodynamics plays a defining role. Ferrari's forms are not drawn and then tested; they are developed alongside airflow. The wind tunnel at Maranello—designed by Renzo Piano—is as central to design as the sketchbook. Here, beauty and performance are reconciled through evidence rather than assumption.

Inside, the same philosophy applies. Ferrari interiors are not about excess or isolation. They are about focus. As technology advances, the challenge is not adding features, but integrating them without distraction. Human–machine interaction has become as critical as materials and craftsmanship.

No Ferrari is complete until it becomes personal. Limited production allows owners to engage directly with the design process, shaping colors, finishes, and details. Individuality, here, is not contradiction—it is fulfillment.

ANY DISCUSSION OF FERRARI DESIGN must acknowledge Pininfarina. From 1951 onward, the partnership between Ferrari and Pininfarina defined some of the most enduring automotive forms ever created. It was not a stylistic alliance, but a philosophical one—rooted in proportion, restraint, and purpose.

From the 212 Inter to the 250 GTO, from the Daytona to the Testarossa, Ferrari design has never chased trends. It has pursued clarity.

That pursuit continues in Maranello today—not toward a fixed image of Ferrari, but toward its next expression.

FERRARI'S V12 ENGINES

"AERODYNAMICS IS COMPENSATION for those who don't know how to squeeze horsepower out of an engine."

— Enzo Ferrari

From the very beginning, Ferrari's identity has been inseparable from the V12 engine. More than a mechanical choice, it was a belief: that performance should be smooth, progressive, and emotionally charged. From the first Ferrari in 1947 to today's most advanced road cars, the V12 has remained the beating heart of the Prancing Horse.

THE STORY BEGINS WITH THE 125 S, Ferrari's first car, powered by a compact V12 designed by Gioachino Colombo. Modest in output but rich in character, it immediately established a philosophy that favored balance and responsiveness over brute force. Early successes confirmed Enzo Ferrari's conviction that twelve cylinders offered not extravagance, but refinement.

That conviction was tested in Formula One. Ferrari's first F1-specific V12 was ambitious but flawed—heavy, complex, and ultimately outpaced by simpler solutions. Yet failure did not deter development. Instead, it refined Ferrari's understanding of what a V12 should be: lighter, more efficient, and increasingly sophisticated.

By the 1950s, Colombo's V12 reached maturity. Twin overhead camshafts, improved breathing, and careful tuning transformed it into a benchmark engine, powering legendary cars such as the 250 GT and the 250 Testa Rossa. Here, Ferrari achieved something rare: engines that dominated on track while remaining usable and charismatic on the road.

The early 1960s elevated the V12 from excellence to myth. In cars like the 250 GTO, the engine became inseparable from form, sound, and sensation. Mechanical harmony defined the experience. As displacement grew and gearboxes evolved, Ferrari refined not only power delivery but comfort and drivability, ensuring performance never came at the expense of control.

By the late 1960s, the front-engined V12 reached its classical peak with the 365 GTB/4 Daytona. Powerful, authoritative, and refined, it marked the end of an era. Yet even before that chapter closed, Ferrari was already looking forward.

ferrari

THE BERLINETTA BOXER of the 1970s reimagined the V12 entirely, placing it mid-mounted for improved balance and handling. This architectural shift preserved Ferrari's signature sound and character while embracing modern performance demands. The concept would evolve into the Testarossa, where function and design merged into an unmistakable visual and mechanical statement.

In the 1990s, Ferrari returned to front-engined V12 grand tourers, combining power with composure. Engines like the F133 series proved that refinement and performance could coexist, earning global recognition and setting new standards for naturally aspirated engines.

The arrival of the F140 family marked another leap. First seen in the Enzo and later refined through models such as the 599, F12berlinetta, and 812 Superfast, it became the most accomplished naturally aspirated V12 Ferrari had ever produced. Its longevity alone speaks to its brilliance.

With LaFerrari, Ferrari proved that tradition and innovation need not conflict. Hybridization enhanced the V12's immediacy without muting its character. Electrification became a tool, not a replacement.

Today, as Ferrari explores an electrified future, the V12 endures in select models—most recently celebrated by the 12Cilindri. It stands as a reminder that some ideas are too fundamental to abandon.

The Ferrari V12 is not nostalgia. It is continuity. A living expression of performance, emotion, and belief—still beating, still evolving, still unmistakably Ferrari.

"THERE'S SOMETHING ABOUT FERRARI THAT GOES BEYOND A CAR. IT'S A BELIEF SYSTEM. AN INSTITUTION. IT'S A PHILOSOPHY AND AN ETHOS"

ACTOR MICHAEL FASSBENDER *in British GQ*

THE CARS

2

FERRARI 125 S (1947)

YEAR INTRODUCED *1947* **ENGINE & CONFIGURATION** *1.5-liter V12* **POWER OUTPUT** *118 Hp* **TOP SPEED** *170 km/h (106 mph)* **NUMBERS BUILT** *2* **PRICE AT LAUNCH** *Not officially listed (factory racing car*

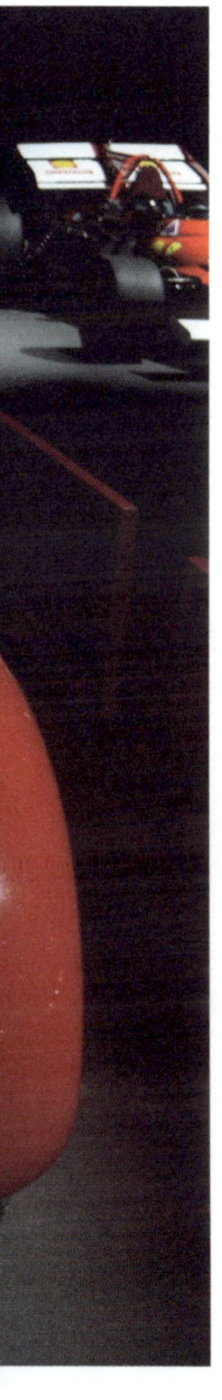

FERRARI 125 S

The Beginning Without Ornament

The Ferrari 125 S was never meant to be admired. It was meant to compete. Built in a post-war Italy defined by scarcity and determination, the car emerged not from luxury ambition but from necessity. Ferrari did not begin as a brand; it began as an idea tested through motion.

Visually, the 125 S is almost severe. Compact proportions, upright stance, and functional bodywork define its presence. There is no attempt at drama. Beauty appears only through balance and intent. Every line exists because it must.

FERRARI 125 S (1947)

Engineering as Belief

At its core sat a small V12 — a bold decision driven not by prestige, but by philosophy. Smaller cylinders, higher revs, smoother response. From the outset, Ferrari chose sensation over simplicity, character over convention.

FERRARI 125 S

Emotion Before Legacy

Driving the 125 S was a conversation, not a performance. Sound, vibration, and movement were immediate and unfiltered. The car demanded commitment and rewarded focus.

Emotionally, the 125 S represents conviction. It is Ferrari before mythology, before status, before expectation. It is the moment Ferrari decided what it stood for — and never deviated.

FERRARI 250 GTO (1962)

YEAR INTRODUCED *1962*   **ENGINE & CONFIGURATION** *3.0-liter V12*   **POWER OUTPUT** *300 hp*
TOP SPEED *280 km/h (174 mph)*   **NUMBERS BUILT** *36*   **PRICE AT LAUNCH** *$18,000*

FERRARI 250 GTO

Form Shaped by Purpose

The Ferrari 250 GTO does not rely on explanation. Its design communicates intent instantly. Long, taut, and disciplined, the body is shaped by airflow and refined by instinct. Nothing is decorative. Nothing is accidental.

The car appears alive even at rest — surfaces held in tension, proportions perfectly resolved. Beauty here is not styled; it emerges.

FERRARI 250 GTO

The Pure Driving State

Inside, the GTO strips the experience to essentials. Thin materials, exposed metal, and a cockpit designed for focus rather than comfort. The driver is not insulated from the machine — they are integrated into it.

Every input matters. Every response feels earned.

FERRARI 250 GTO

When Myth Becomes Meaning

Emotionally, the 250 GTO balances brutality with grace. It is demanding without being hostile, poetic without softness. A racing car that never forgot how to communicate with its driver.

Its cultural significance extends beyond rarity. The GTO belongs to a moment when craftsmanship, regulation, and ambition aligned perfectly — a moment that cannot be repeated.

The 250 GTO is not remembered because it is valuable. It is remembered because it is complete.

FERRARI 250 GT LUSSO (1963)

YEAR INTRODUCED *1963*   ENGINE & CONFIGURATION *3.0-liter V12*   POWER OUTPUT *240 hp*
TOP SPEED *240 km/h (150 mph)*   NUMBERS BUILT *350*   PRICE AT LAUNCH *$13,500*

FERRARI 250 GT LUSSO

Elegance Without Effort

The Ferrari 250 GT Lusso represents a quieter kind of confidence.
It does not chase speed through aggression or excess. Instead, it
achieves distinction through proportion, restraint, and balance.
Among Ferrari's many expressions of performance, the Lusso
stands apart as the most composed.

Its design is remarkably pure. The roofline flows gently into the
rear, the glasshouse feels light, and the long hood stretches forward
with calm assurance. Nothing interrupts the silhouette. The Lusso
does not announce itself; it invites closer attention.

FERRARI 250 GT LUSSO

Performance as Refinement

Unlike Ferrari's racing-derived models, the Lusso was designed for distance rather than domination. It carries speed with ease, not tension. This sense of effortlessness defines the car's character. Performance is present, but never theatrical.
Inside, the cabin reinforces this philosophy. Leather surfaces, thoughtful detailing, and an airy feel create an environment that feels human and welcoming. It is not indulgent, but considered — a place designed for hours behind the wheel rather than moments of spectacle.

625
625
PRX 932B
HUBLOT

FERRARI 250 GT LUSSO

A Philosophy in Aluminum

Emotionally, the Lusso represents Ferrari at its most mature. It proves that excitement does not require aggression, and that beauty can emerge from knowing when to stop. In Ferrari's lineage, the Lusso is a moment of calm perfection — a reminder that restraint can be as powerful as excess.

FERRARI 365 GTB/4 "DAYTONA" (1968)

YEAR INTRODUCED *1968*   **ENGINE & CONFIGURATION** *4.4-liter V12*   **POWER OUTPUT** *352 hp*
TOP SPEED *280 km/h (174 mph)*   **NUMBERS BUILT** *1,284 coupes*   **PRICE AT LAUNCH** *$19,500*

FERRARI 365 GTB/4 "DAYTONA"

Power with Authority

The Ferrari Daytona is a car defined by presence. Where earlier Ferraris expressed elegance, the Daytona asserts confidence. Its long hood, wide stance, and clean, angular lines signal strength without theatrics. This is not a romantic Ferrari — it is a decisive one.
The proportions are unmistakably front-engine grand tourer: cabin pushed rearward, engine stretched ahead, and a rear that feels planted and resolved. The design feels serious, purposeful, and assured.

Km/h
300
LUCI
AMPERE
LIGHTS

FERRARI 365 GTB/4 "DAYTONA"

The Analog Ideal

Inside, the Daytona remains firmly rooted in the mechanical era.
Large gauges, tactile controls, and a direct driving position place
the driver at the center of the experience. There is no mediation, no
abstraction — only connection.
Driving the Daytona feels deliberate. Inputs are weighted, responses immediate. It is a car that rewards intent rather than aggression.

FERRARI 365 GTB/4 "DAYTONA"

The End of a Chapter

Emotionally, the Daytona carries the weight of finality. It represents the culmination of Ferrari's classic front-engine V12 philosophy, perfected just before the world moved on. Soon, mid-engine layouts would redefine performance, making the Daytona both a peak and a conclusion.

Today, it stands as a monument to authority and clarity — a Ferrari that knew exactly what it was, and closed its chapter without compromise.

FERRARI 308 GTB (1975)

YEAR INTRODUCED *1975*   **ENGINE & CONFIGURATION** *2.9-liter V8*   **POWER OUTPUT** *255 hp*   **TOP SPEED** *252 km/h (157 mph)*   **NUMBERS BUILT** *12,000 (GTB/GTS combined)*   **PRICE AT LAUNCH** *$29,000*

FERRARI 308 GTB

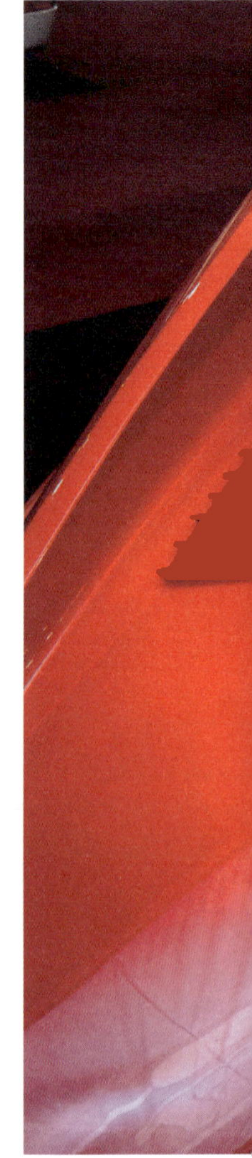

A New Kind of Accessibility

The Ferrari 308 GTB arrived at a moment when the idea of the exotic sports car was being questioned. Regulations tightened, fuel concerns loomed, and excess no longer felt inevitable. Ferrari's response was not retreat, but refinement.
Visually, the 308 GTB is defined by balance. Its mid-engine proportions are compact and harmonious, with a low nose, flowing roofline, and subtly flared rear. Nothing feels exaggerated. The design is confident without being confrontational — elegant, legible, and unmistakably Italian.

Ferrari

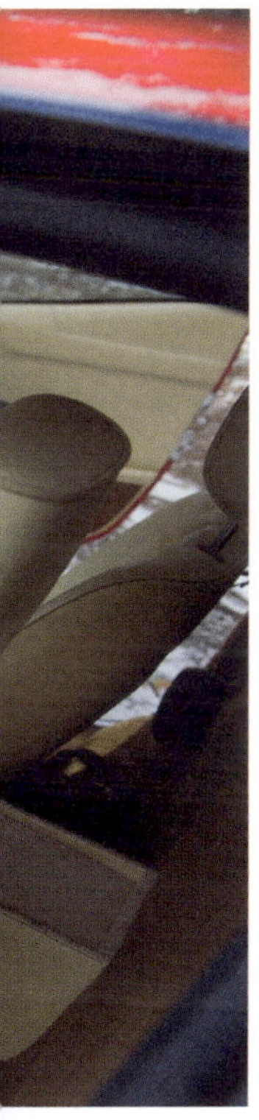

FERRARI 308 GTB

Performance Made Human

Unlike Ferrari's larger, more demanding machines, the 308 feels approachable. The cabin wraps gently around the driver, controls fall naturally to hand, and visibility is unusually generous for a Ferrari. This is a car designed to be driven often, not just admired.
The experience is intimate rather than intimidating. Speed builds progressively, communication is constant, and the car feels light on its feet. Emotion comes not from spectacle, but from connection.

FERRARI 308 GTB

The Ferrari of Imagination

Culturally, the 308 GTB became the Ferrari people dreamed of. It lived
on posters, screens, and in collective imagination. More importantly,
it defined a template — the mid-engine V8 Ferrari — that would shape
the brand for decades.
The 308 GTB is remembered not because it shouted, but because it
spoke clearly. It made Ferrari feel closer, without ever feeling ordinary.

308

FERRARI TESTAROSSA (1984)

YEAR INTRODUCED *1984* **ENGINE & CONFIGURATION** *4.9-liter flat-12* **POWER OUTPUT** *390 hp*
TOP SPEED *290 km/h (180 mph)* **NUMBERS BUILT** *9,900* **PRICE AT LAUNCH** *$85,000*

FERRARI TESTAROSSA

Design as Declaration

If the 308 GTB refined Ferrari's image, the Testarossa exploded it.
This was not a car designed to blend in or soften its message. It was
built to be seen — and remembered.
Wide, dramatic, and instantly recognizable, the Testarossa's proportions defied convention. Its side strakes, born from engineering
necessity, became architectural statements. The car's width and
horizontal emphasis give it an almost monumental presence.

FERRARI TESTAROSSA

An Era Captured in Form

The Testarossa is inseparable from its time — and that is its strength. It captures the spirit of an era with absolute clarity, turning excess into identity.

In Ferrari's history, the Testarossa stands as proof that boldness, when executed with conviction, can become timeless in its own way.

testarossa

FERRARI TESTAROSSA

Confidence Without Apology

Inside, the Testarossa feels expansive rather than intimate. Broad surfaces, strong geometry, and a sense of space reflect the confidence of its era. This is not a cockpit designed to disappear around the driver — it is part of the performance.

Emotionally, the Testarossa is about arrival. It represents success, ambition, and visibility. It does not seek subtlety, because subtlety was never the point.

FERRARI F40 (1987)

YEAR INTRODUCED *1987*   **ENGINE & CONFIGURATION** *2.9-liter twin-turbo V8*   **POWER OUTPUT** *478 hp*
TOP SPEED *324 km/h (201 mph)*   **NUMBERS BUILT** *1,315*   **PRICE AT LAUNCH** *$400,000*

FERRARI F40

The Refusal to Soften

The Ferrari F40 was created as a celebration, but it reads like a challenge. At a time when comfort and electronics were beginning to reshape performance cars, Ferrari chose defiance. The F40 strips the idea of a supercar down to its most uncompromising form. Visually, it is raw and unapologetic. Sharp edges, exposed fasteners, and functional openings dominate the design. The towering rear wing is not an aesthetic flourish; it is a statement of intent. Beauty here is a consequence of purpose, not a goal in itself.

FERRARI F40

Driving Without Filters

Inside, the F40 rejects luxury entirely. Bare carbon fiber, minimal trim, and exposed structure define the cabin. There is no attempt to shield the driver from noise, heat, or effort. Everything is immediate. Emotionally, the F40 is demanding and vulnerable. It does not correct mistakes or soften responses. It rewards skill and punishes complacency. This honesty is precisely why it endures.
The F40 is remembered not as a product of its time, but as a refusal to follow it. It is Ferrari at its most truthful.

FERRARI ENZO (2002)

YEAR INTRODUCED *2002*   **ENGINE & CONFIGURATION** *6.0-liter V12*   **POWER OUTPUT** *651 hp*
TOP SPEED *355 km/h (221 mph)*   **NUMBERS BUILT** *400*   **PRICE AT LAUNCH** *$650,000*

FERRARI ENZO

Performance Through Precision

Named after the founder of Ferrari, the Enzo marked a decisive shift. Where earlier icons relied on raw sensation, the Enzo embraced technology as the path forward.
Its design is sharp, angular, and unapologetically technical. Every surface is shaped by aerodynamics and cooling requirements. Elegance gives way to efficiency, and the car makes no attempt to disguise that priority.

FERRARI ENZO

The Digital Threshold

Inside, the Enzo feels closer to a race car than a road car. The cockpit is sparse, focused, and dominated by function. Paddle shifters, digital displays, and driver aids transform the experience from physical dialogue to calculated performance.

Emotionally, the Enzo overwhelms through capability rather than chaos. Speed arrives with composure. Control replaces drama.

The Enzo stands as a bridge — between Ferrari's analog past and its data-driven future. It is not nostalgic, but it is essential.

LF54 ASO

FERRARI LAFERRARI (2013)

YEAR INTRODUCED *2013* **ENGINE & CONFIGURATION** *6.3-liter V12 + HY-KERS hybrid*
POWER OUTPUT *950 hp (combined)* **TOP SPEED** *Over 350 km/h (217+ mph)*
NUMBERS BUILT *499 coupes (+210 Aperta)* **PRICE AT LAUNCH** *$1.4 million*

FERRARI LAFERRARI

Redefining Performance

LaFerrari arrived at a moment when Ferrari needed to prove that
progress did not mean dilution. Electrification was no longer
theoretical — it was inevitable. What Ferrari delivered was not
compromise, but amplification.

Visually, LaFerrari is disciplined rather than dramatic. Its form is
complex yet controlled, shaped by airflow and intent rather than
nostalgia. There are no theatrical wings, no exaggerated gestures.
Presence comes from proportion and precision. The car looks intel-
ligent — fast because it understands speed.

FERRARI LAFERRARI

Emotion, Intensified

Inside, the cockpit feels immersive and purposeful. Digital interfaces replace analog tradition, yet the experience remains physical and focused. The driver sits at the center of the system, not separated from it.

Emotionally, LaFerrari redefines sensation. The hybrid system sharpens response, filling every gap with immediacy. Acceleration feels continuous, relentless, and deeply engaging. Rather than masking the combustion engine's character, electrification heightens it. LaFerrari matters because it reframed the conversation. It proved that Ferrari could evolve without losing identity — that emotion could be engineered, not erased. It is not a farewell to the past, but a confident step beyond it.

FERRARI LAFERRARI

FERRARI DAYTONA SP3 (2022)

YEAR INTRODUCED *2022*   **ENGINE & CONFIGURATION** *6.5-liter naturally aspirated V12*
POWER OUTPUT *829 hp*   **TOP SPEED** *Over 340 km/h (211+ mph)*   **NUMBERS BUILT** *599*
PRICE AT LAUNCH *$2.25 million*

FERRARI DAYTONA SP3

Looking Back Without Nostalgia

The Daytona SP3 is Ferrari reflecting on its past — not with sentimentality, but with clarity. Inspired by endurance racers of the 1960s, it does not replicate history. It interprets it.
The design is sculptural and restrained. Clean surfaces replace aggression, and volume replaces ornament. The dramatic rear treatment is both functional and symbolic, recalling prototype racers without imitation. The SP3 feels carved, architectural, and deliberate.

FERRARI DAYTONA SP3

A Celebration of Sound

Inside, the experience is modern but focused. Digital elements coexist with tactile controls, maintaining a sense of engagement rather than spectacle. Everything serves the act of driving. Emotionally, the SP3 is about presence. In an era defined by electrification, it celebrates the naturally aspirated V12 as an event — the build of sound, the rise in intensity, the physicality of response. It is not faster because of novelty, but because of refinement.

The Daytona SP3 stands as a statement of confidence. Ferrari does not abandon its heritage, nor does it cling to it. Instead, it carries it forward — alive, relevant, and unmistakably Ferrari.

إذا كنت تقدر على الحلم،
فأنت قادر على تحقيقه.
IF YOU CAN DREAM,
YOU CAN DO IT.

FERRARI F80

YEAR INTRODUCED *TBA*   **ENGINE & CONFIGURATION** *Expected hybrid V8*   **POWER OUTPUT** *Estimated 1,000+ hp*   **TOP SPEED** *TBA*   **NUMBERS BUILT** *TBA*   **PRICE AT LAUNCH** *$3–4 million*

FERRARI F80

A Question, Not a Promise

The Ferrari F80 was never intended to become a production car
— and that is precisely its strength. Free from regulation, market
demands, and practicality, it exists as a pure act of exploration. The
F80 does not announce what Ferrari will build. It asks what Ferrari
could be.

Visually, the F80 is uncompromising. Sharp, intersecting surfaces
replace traditional curves, and the car appears carved rather than
shaped. Proportions are extreme: a compact cockpit pushed forward, an expansive rear dominated by structure and force. Negative
space is as important as mass, creating tension rather than balance.
This is not classical beauty. It is architectural, aggressive, and inten-
tional. The F80 does not seek to please — it seeks to provoke.

FERRARI F80

Ferrari Without Nostalgia

Unlike many future-facing concepts, the F80 resists heritage cues. There are no visual quotations, no retro gestures. Instead, Ferrari's identity emerges through philosophy rather than form: focus on the driver, clarity of purpose, and emotion born from performance. Inside, the imagined cockpit is stripped and immersive. Digital interfaces dominate, physical controls are minimal, and the driver is positioned as part of the machine rather than a passenger within it. The experience is intense, concentrated, and unapologetically forward-looking.

Emotionally, the F80 represents Ferrari thinking aloud. It is the brand testing its own boundaries, questioning how far form and function can evolve without losing soul. In that sense, it mirrors Ferrari's earliest cars — driven by conviction rather than consensus. The F80 may never turn a wheel, but its importance lies elsewhere. It expands imagination. It proves that Ferrari's future is not limited by its past — only informed by it.

In a lineage defined by motion, the F80 stands still — and asks the next question.

FERRARI F80

“WHY FERRARI?
IF YOU SAW ONE
ON THE MOTOR-
WAY WHEN YOU
WERE FIVE OR
SIX, YOU NEVER
FORGOT IT …
MY DREAM WAS
TO WIN THREE
MICHELIN
STARS AND OWN
A FERRARI.”

CHEF GORDON RAMSEY *in British GQ*

TCA
TELEVISION CRITICS ASSOCIATION
FOX

THE BRAN

3

MATT DAMON   CHRISTIAN BALE
FORD v FERRARI
NOVEMBER 15
#FORDVFERRARI
WWW.FORDVFERRARI.COM
IMAX

FERRARI IN POPULAR CULTURE

SOME BRANDS SEEK VISIBILITY. FERRARI ACCUMULATES MEANING.

In popular culture, Ferrari does not function as product placement in the conventional sense. It appears not because it needs exposure, but because it already carries symbolism. Speed, elegance, ambition, danger, excess—Ferrari communicates all of this instantly, without explanation. That is the essence of soft power: influence exercised through recognition rather than persuasion.

ACROSS DECADES, FERRARI HAS BECOME a visual shorthand. Filmmakers, musicians, and game designers return to it not for novelty, but for clarity. A Ferrari on screen signals intent before a character speaks. It frames identity.

Cinema has been one of Ferrari's most powerful amplifiers. In Ford v Ferrari (released internationally as Le Mans '66), Ferrari is not simply a backdrop, but the axis around which the story turns. The film dramatizes the rivalry between Enzo Ferrari and Ford, using the 1966 24 Hours of Le Mans as its climax. Here, Ferrari represents tradition, pride, and uncompromising vision—an antagonist defined not by malice, but by conviction.

A very different portrait appears in Ferrari, which turns inward. Set against the 1957 Mille Miglia, the film focuses less on victory than on fragility: grief, pressure, and personal cost. Ferrari's cars remain powerful and beautiful, but the tone is restrained, even melancholic. The myth is not dismantled—it is humanized.

NEON
ADAM DRIVER   PENÉLOPE CRUZ   SHAILENE WOODLEY
531
533
A MICHAEL MANN FILM
FERRARI
DECEMBER 25
WRITTEN BY
TROY
KENNEDY MARTIN
DIRECTED BY
MICHAEL
MANN
R

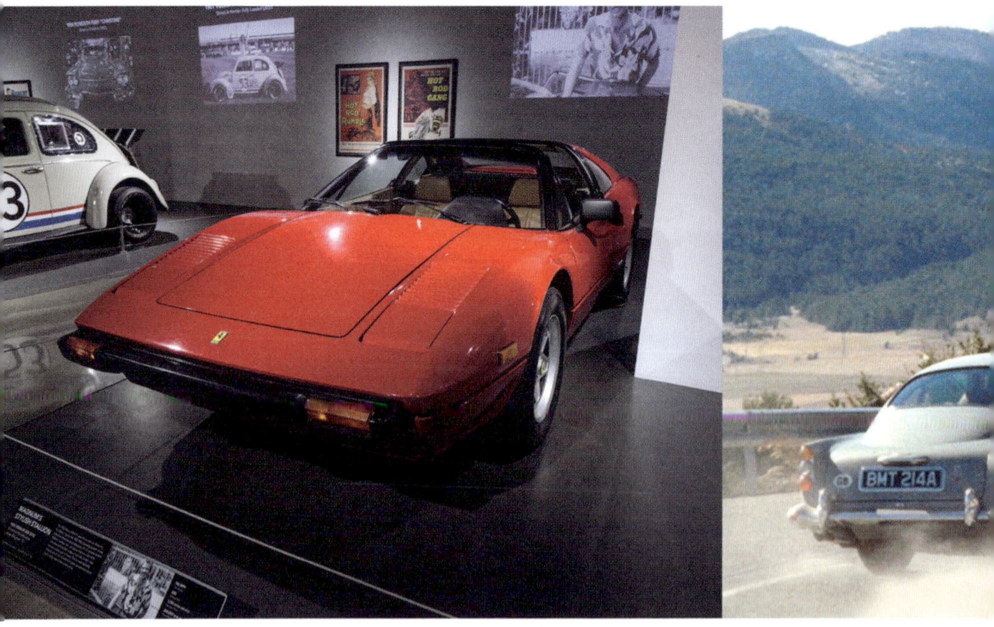

MAGNUM P.I.
1982 Ferrari 308 GTSi
driven by Tom Selleck in
Magnum P.I

OFTEN, A FERRARI NEEDS NO NARRATIVE FOCUS to dominate a scene. In GoldenEye, the Ferrari F355 driven by Xenia Onatopp becomes an extension of character. Color, speed, and danger align perfectly. The car communicates seduction and threat more efficiently than dialogue ever could.

Television has reinforced Ferrari's cultural permanence. In Magnum, P.I., Ferrari's 308 models became inseparable from the show's relaxed yet aspirational tone. Similarly, Miami Vice transformed the Ferrari Testarossa into an icon of 1980s excess—white bodywork cutting through neon-lit streets, embodying speed, style, and moral ambiguity.

Ferrari's symbolism extends even into stories of crime and power. In Narcos, Ferraris signify dominance and untouchability, reinforc-

ing how deeply the brand is associated with success—legitimate or otherwise.

In the digital realm, Ferrari's influence continues. Video games such as Gran Turismo treat Ferrari with reverence, often positioning its cars as benchmarks of performance and design. In 2021, even Fortnite introduced a drivable Ferrari, confirming the brand's reach across generations and formats.

Ferrari's presence in popular culture is not accidental, nor is it static. Each appearance adds a layer, reinforcing the idea that Ferrari is not merely a car, but a symbol—one flexible enough to mean many things, yet precise enough to always be recognizable.

That is Ferrari's enduring soft power: never imposed, always understood.

PAUL NEWMAN

FAMOUS
FERRARI OWNERS

FOR SOME, FERRARI IS ADMIRED FROM A DISTANCE—through racing history, engineering excellence, or design. For others, it becomes something more intimate. In the hands of cultural icons, Ferrari often functions as an extension of identity: a projection of values, ambition, and self-image.

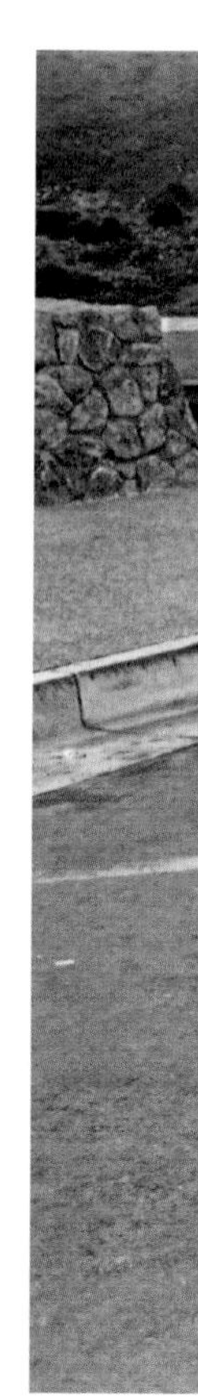

FEW FIGURES EMBODY THIS MORE CLEARLY than Steve Mc-
Queen. Known as the "King of Cool," McQueen pursued racing with
the seriousness of a professional, even competing under a pseudo-
nym. His relationship with Ferrari was instinctive rather than stra-
tegic. Cars such as the 250 GT Lusso and the 275 GTB/4 reflected his
preference for understatement paired with capability. Even his ec-
centric modifications spoke to authenticity rather than display. For
McQueen, Ferrari was not a trophy—it was a tool.

A similar seriousness defined Paul Newman, whose devotion to
motorsport extended far beyond celebrity fascination. Racing for
decades, Newman approached driving with discipline and humili-
ty. His association with Ferrari was brief but meaningful, including
early competition use of a 308 GTB. In Newman's world, Ferrari be-
longed to the same category as racing itself: demanding, honest, and
earned.

ONE-OFF

IN MUSIC, FERRARI HAS OFTEN REPRESENTED MASTERY rather than excess. Guitarist Eric Clapton built one of the most discerning Ferrari collections, centered around timeless models such as the 250 GT Lusso. His collaboration with Ferrari on the bespoke SP12 EC underscored a shared respect for craftsmanship. For Clapton, Ferrari was not spectacle—it was resonance.

In contrast, global sports icons like Michael Jordan embraced Ferrari as a symbol of dominance. His ownership of multiple Testarossas and later grand tourers reflected success at its most visible. Yet even here, Ferrari functioned less as ornament and more as confirmation—a physical expression of achievement already earned.

CINEMA'S MOST IMPOSING FIGURES, INCLUDING Arnold Schwarzenegger and Sylvester Stallone, likewise gravitated toward Ferrari's blend of power and authority. Their choices reinforced Ferrari's role as a shorthand for strength, ambition, and presence.

Perhaps the most poetic relationship belongs to Miles Davis. When Davis returned from a period of illness and silence, he marked the moment not only with music, but with a bright yellow Ferrari. Arriving in it was not vanity—it was declaration. Ferrari, here, became proof of survival and creative rebirth.

In contemporary culture, Ferrari has taken on new meanings. In hip-hop, artists such as Jay-Z use Ferrari imagery as shorthand for ascent, autonomy, and control. The car's symbolism is instantly legible: arrival without explanation.

Yet Ferrari's exclusivity remains carefully guarded. Stories of rejected buyers and quiet blacklists—whether real or exaggerated—reinforce the idea that Ferrari ownership is not purely transactional. It is selective, curated, and conditional.

Across generations and disciplines, Ferrari ownership has never meant just possession. It has meant alignment. For those behind the wheel, the Prancing Horse becomes a mirror—reflecting not only success, but how that success is understood.

That is Ferrari's enduring appeal: not as a reward, but as an identity claimed.

"YOU BUY A FERRARI WHEN YOU WANT TO BE SOMEBODY."

MUSICIAN FRANK SINATRA *in New York Times.*

THE END

FERRARI TESTAROSSA

THANK YOU, FERRARI

FERRARI HAS NEVER BEEN ABOUT STANDING STILL or getting everything perfect. It has always been about moving forward.

Over the years, shapes have changed, technology has advanced, and ideas of performance have evolved. But the heart of Ferrari has stayed the same: building cars that do more than go fast—cars that carry feeling, intention, and personality every time they move.

THE TEN CARS IN THIS BOOK ARE NOT IMPORTANT simply because they were the fastest or the rarest. They matter because each one marks a choice. A moment when Ferrari followed belief instead of convenience, when design served purpose, and emotion was never left behind.

Ferrari's story is not a straight path. It moves from simple beginnings to bold statements, from raw, mechanical honesty to refined digital precision. Each era adds its own voice, its own character, its own way of understanding speed and beauty.

What remains constant is not nostalgia or technology, but a simple idea: that a car can still make us feel something real.That idea is Ferrari's true legacy—and it is still being written.

"WHEN YOU BUY ME, YOU ARE BUYING A FERRARI. IF YOU DRIVE A FERRARI, … YOU HIT THE MOTORWAY, AND YOU STEP ON THE GAS."

CREDITS

Helmin Publishing would like to thank the following for permission to use images in this book.

2-3	Roland Woon	Shutterstock.com
10	GPL-Fred Taylor	Alamy.com
12	The Picture Art Collection	Alamy.com
13	Phil Talbot	Alamy.com
14	trabantos	Shutterstock.com
16	eliscora	Shutterstock.com
17	Wirestock Creators	Shutterstock.com
19	Dmitry Eagle Orlov	Shutterstock.com
20	JoshBryan	Shutterstock.com
23	Fyuzu	Shutterstock.com
24	Piotr Piatrouski	Shutterstock.com
27	Debby Wong	Shutterstock.com
30-31	Dan74	Shutterstock.com
32	Mau47	Shutterstock.com
35	Krzysztof Dzidek	Shutterstock.com
36	Karolis Kavolelis	Shutterstock.com
38-39	Paul Pollock	Shutterstock.com
41	EA Photography	Shutterstock.com
42-43	D. Ribeiro	Shutterstock.com
44-45	Dan74	Shutterstock.com
46-47	FernandoV	Shutterstock.com
48	FernandoV	Shutterstock.com
50-51	FernandoV	Shutterstock.com
52	Luca85	Shutterstock.com
54-55	Phil Talbot	Alamy.com
56-57	Antonin Vincent	DPPI
58	FernandoV	Shutterstock.com
61	FernandoV	Shutterstock.com
62-63	Martin Brazill	Shutterstock.com
65	Sergey Kohl	Shutterstock.com
66	FernandoV	Shutterstock.com
69	S.Candide	Shutterstock.com
70-71	Adomas Daunoravicius	Shutterstock.com
72	byruineves	Shutterstock.com
75	byruineves	Shutterstock.com
76-77	Zuumy	Shutterstock.com
78-79	Zuumy	Shutterstock.com